Living with TEENS

A PARENT'S HANDBOOK

HOWARD R. BINGHAM

Deseret Book Company
Salt Lake City, Utah

©1983 Deseret Book Company
All rights reserved
Printed in the United States of America
First printing September 1983
Library of Congress Catalog Card No. 83-72479
ISBN 0-87747-956-9

*To Joan, my wife, who did most of the work of
raising our teenagers;*

*Michele, our first teenager, who gave me
some very helpful, constructive criticism
on the ideas contained in these pages; and*

*Corey, Janet, Tamara, and Suzanne, who,
with Michele, have been the superstars
in our game of life.*

Contents

Preface

Teenagers can be beautiful or homely, fun to be with or exasperating, happy or sad, teachable or stubborn. They come in all sizes, shapes, and types. No two are alike!

Through all their differences, however, there is one unifying sameness: they are all in the process of *becoming*. During the formative years between twelve and twenty, the process is not the easiest thing in the world for either the teenagers or their parents and others who associate with them. But neither is it hopeless.

I believe that this sameness among teenagers allows us as parents to establish some common principles and procedures that might be applied to rearing *any* teenager. Thus, I refer to this small volume as a handbook for parents, and from that perspective, I suggest that you use it as a handbook. That is, don't simply read it once and then put it away on a shelf. Rather, test each idea long enough to give it a fair trial, and come back to the book often until you have mastered its principles. You may make adjustments in the way you deal with your teenager to fit your own personality, family situation, and relationship with him. As you put these principles to practical use, refer to the text occasionally to be sure you are making a genuine attempt to implement them before you revise or reject them.

In this book, I generally use the word *him* in referring to the teenager, but I also mean *her*. The masculine pronoun has been used only for ease in writing. Names and details have been changed in personal experiences to avoid embarrassing those who have shared with me their successes and failures in rearing teenagers. And finally, though I am addressing my discussion to you as a parent, I want you to know that I myself am included in this discussion—we parents are all in this together.

1

From
Terrible
Teen
to Human
Being

Perhaps you're the parent of one or more teenagers, and you're concerned about how well you're handling that relationship.

Or perhaps you're the parent of a handsome, adorable, unspoiled ten-year-old son, and you're worried because you know that one day soon he'll turn into a teenager.

Or perhaps you're a man who recently married an attractive widow with three gangly, pimply creatures between the ages of twelve and twenty, and becoming an "instant" father—especially a father of teenagers—frightens you.

Or perhaps you are a widow, and no man will call you for a second date because you have teenage children.

Whatever your role—husband, wife, or single parent—if you are responsible for some part or all of the upbringing of a teenager, don't despair. There is hope!

Somewhere in the far reaches of time, you yourself were once a teenager. We all were, though it may be difficult for some parents to remember that. Sometimes as parents watch teenagers get themselves into and out of all kinds of trouble, causing difficulties for others and being generally impossible to live with, they declare, "I was never like that!" However, probably few of us could get away with that statement in the presence of our own parents.

Although I sympathize with those who look upon all teenagers as difficult to get along with, as impossible to reason with, or even as not worth working with, I personally feel that teenagers are terrific people. And I speak from experience, for I have been called "Dad" by five of them. I realize that I'm somewhat prejudiced and that my own terrific kids might be considered only average by someone else. But however terrific or even average they may be, they didn't get that way by accident. They, like most other teenagers, have presented many problems to us as parents that have required careful handling and understanding.

If you haven't already had problems with your teenagers that have left you gasping for breath or scratching your head in bewilderment, just be patient—you will. Problems seem to come with the territory. And sometimes the problems come in bunches, often before parents expect them or are prepared to deal with them. Some of the problems are relatively easy to handle; others may be more difficult. In general, they may relate to

1. Demands for independence
2. The need to be like peers
3. Too much success or failure with athletics or other competitive activities
4. Too much success or failure with relationships with members of the opposite sex
5. Self-consciousness as a result of the many changes that come with puberty
6. Experimentation with tobacco, liquor, drugs, or other harmful substances

7. Experimentation with sex

At some point during your child's teenage years, you may almost reach a point at which "jumping ship" seems the only viable alternative. However close you may be to that point, however, you must not—you cannot—give up.

Fortunately, the condition is not permanent. About the time the teenager approaches adulthood, the problems seem to diminish and he's better able to handle them in a responsible way. But if the problems or the symptoms are not dealt with constructively during the earlier years, they can leave permanent scars, often on the teen's self-image. That kind of scar cannot be removed by surgery, but it can be avoided with some basic preventive techniques applied by parents in the daily processes of living with him. The essential point is for each parent to want to make something positive out of life with his teenager.

2

Loving Them (Whether You Like Them or Not)

It's not always easy to love teenagers. Some of them seem determined to guarantee that we won't. Teenagers have been known to use every disagreeable device imaginable to alienate adults. Parents who don't fall for such ploys—who love the teenagers anyway, despite their exasperating ways—can in turn be loved and respected by these unpredictable persons. All teenagers want and need to be both liked and loved.

On close examination, you may find that you

love your teenager only for what he might become, or simply because he's yours, or because you know you *ought* to love him. But he deserves more than that—he deserves your complete, unconditional love. And this can be developed and nourished, if you really work at it and have a positive attitude. You need to make every effort to keep telling him that you love him, and to show by your every word and expression that you mean what you say. If you do this, ultimately you'll find that it's true—you really *do* love him.

Some people claim that talking to houseplants in sweet, positive tones and praising and encouraging them will cause them to grow and thrive. Now that may well be foolish as far as plants are concerned, but as it pertains to teenagers, it's absolutely true. Those who are addressed and encouraged positively will grow and thrive in positive ways. Sometimes it takes time on the part of both the parent and the teenager, but it's a goal well worth striving for.

If you criticize your teenager or constantly nag him, he's going to react, and probably negatively. Perhaps he'll completely turn you off and tune you out, or he may react just the opposite and fight back. Either reaction is counterproductive, as parents find out rather quickly.

If you're going to get results in communicating with your teenager, make your criticisms and directions to him constructive and positive. Praise him and show a positive, consistent interest in what he finds interesting. This will lead you to the real person inside.

If in the past you have not praised and complimented him consistently, be patient and keep trying. It will take some time to build your relationship and bring him to the point where he trusts you and your motives. He may be suspicious at first, wondering if you can really change so much. You might have to work at it for some time before he recognizes that your praise and concern are genuine.

Everyone has some quality, talent, or ability that is praiseworthy. Find out what special talents and abilities your teenager has, and praise him for these things often and sincerely. If you persist, the results will eventually be positive, and your relationship will move forward.

An illustration of this principle may be found in the experience of Mike, a high school junior. He had a reputation as a fighter—he'd take on anyone, any size, youth or teacher, for any reason or for no reason at all. He seemed to be constantly listening for an offensive remark as an excuse for picking a fight. Should anyone make such a mistake, Mike would first issue threats, thus providing a period of fearful anticipation for his intended victim. Then he would appoint a time and place for "having it out." If the intended victim failed to show, Mike would ambush him somewhere else.

Often bullies are all threat with no follow-through. Not Mike. He was a good fighter, and he almost always won his fights. Though he was of average size, he was strong and quick. He feared no one, and his successes gave him feelings of confidence.

In school Mike often baited teachers with surly or disrespectful behavior, apparently hoping to goad one of them into a fight. Once he succeeded. A history teacher took the bait. He calmly placed his arm around Mike's shoulder and said, "I'll see you after school in the gym."

The teacher brought boxing gloves, and that afternoon the two of them, about equal in size, squared off. A good bout followed, as each landed solid blows and both ended up exhausted. Then they shook hands and went their separate ways.

After school the next day, Mike lingered near the history teacher's room. They started talking together, the first of many conversations. The teacher became aware of Mike's special interests and abilities and encouraged him in them. As his interest in Mike increased, the number of fights Mike engaged in decreased. The two became close friends, and Mike began to think about his future.

Before his senior year ended, Mike had stopped fighting and had become a good citizen in the classroom.

Let's review briefly the history teacher's method of working with Mike:

1. Get his attention.
2. Earn his respect.
3. Accept him as he is.
4. Communicate with him.
5. Learn about his interests and strengths.
6. Encourage him in them.
7. Treat him as an adult, not as a child.
8. Let him know of your feelings for him.

The teacher was able to reach Mike and do what Mike's parents had *not* done. By following a similar "plan of attack," perhaps they could have reached him and prevented the necessity of help from a surrogate parent, the teacher. The method the teacher used works well for parents and for all who deal with teenagers.

If you haven't been in the habit of giving your teenager hugs and pats on the back, it's not too late to start. And if you've started, don't stop just because he's taller than you are! Words and affection are essential to the survival of human beings—including teenagers.

Clinical experiments have shown that children often wither and waste away when they are denied caresses and the soothing influence of the human voice. Put your arms around your teenager. Kiss him. Pat him on the back, both physically and verbally. Make positive statements about him to others and to him personally. These are the best medicine for nearly all teenage ailments.

Volumes have been written on the subject of love, as writers have tried to identify different kinds of love—from erotic to philanthropic. The love of parents for their children lies somewhere between these extremes. Families differ one from another in the kind of love the individuals show for each other and in the intensity of that love. But one element of love is important—even essential—in every parent-child relationship. That element is described by the word *unconditional*. This means that you love your child absolutely, with no qualifications, regardless of his behavior or any character trait or problem he might have that others might criticize or think about negatively.

Unconditional love means you can "hate the sin but love the sinner." It means separating his misdeeds from his worth as a unique individual, a child of God. It means applying discipline for his misbehavior one moment and, at the next moment, putting your arm around him and telling him you love him. This is absolutely essential to his well-being as well as to your effectiveness as a parent.

How can you show unconditional love toward your teenager? The following story illustrates this principle.

Joe, seventeen, was enjoying his summer vacation before his senior year of high school. He had just left his girl friend's home and was driving home in his father's nearly new car.

Mrs. James was coming down another street at the same time, also driving a nearly new car. They reached the unmarked intersection simultaneously, and neither saw the other approach because high bushes blocked their view. Since they were in an area that saw little traffic, they were both probably driving a little too fast. The crash was inevitable, and both cars were totaled, but the drivers, fortunately, were only shaken up.

Someone in the neighborhood witnessed the accident and went to a nearby home to call the police and Joe's parents. As they waited, Mrs. James heard Joe repeat again and again, with great anguish, "My dad will kill me!" She found herself hoping his mother would arrive first.

Within a few minutes Joe's father arrived. He leaped from his car and strode rapidly toward his son. Mrs. James's heart pounded as she waited for the father's reaction to the accident. Imagine her relief—and surprise—when the father rushed to Joe, threw his arms around him, and said, "It's all right, son. I'm glad you're okay."

Both Joe and his father knew something about unconditional love, and onlookers that day learned a valuable lesson.

3

Having
Fun
With
Them

Has your teenager ever seen you laugh? Has he seen you laugh at yourself? Does he know that you are human and that you don't really think you know everything?

If you hope to improve your relationship, you must help him to see the full breadth of your personality, including your ability to see the lighter side of life. And you must be able to see the full breadth of *his* personality as well.

Most parents believe they know their children better than anyone else knows them. Yet in new situations they often discover facets of their children's personalities that surprise them. Having a good sense of humor can help ease tension in many otherwise tense situations.

As you work to develop your relationship with your teenager, encourage him to share things that he enjoys doing. Learn to relax with him. Put aside the lectures, discipline, and chores occasionally, and just have fun.

In a relaxed atmosphere, let him get acquainted with the side of you that causes your friends to like you. As he learns to like you rather than fear you or simply respect (or resent) your authority, you'll find your role as parent becoming easier to fulfill and even more fun.

Conversely, make a real and genuine effort to get better acquainted with the side of him that causes *his* friends to like *him*. As you learn to like and accept him more readily, you'll find the barriers between you starting to fall and your relationship improving.

Virginia Miller had trouble understanding her oldest daughter, Ginny. When she herself was in college, Virginia had wanted very much to be popular, but she was never nominated for an office or asked to run for homecoming queen. Now she was anxious that her daughter not miss out on the popularity she had missed. She wanted Ginny to "be somebody."

Ginny was quite attractive as she entered high school, but to her mother's dismay, she preferred studying bugs to trying out for cheerleader or running for office. She was more interested in biology field trips than attending football games.

As Ginny's high school years sped by, she became increasingly attractive, but also increasingly shy and retiring. Her mother, unwilling to accept her as she was, attempted to push Ginny into social activities, but Ginny refused to be pushed. A gulf developed between them.

Frustrated, Virginia went to her husband and cried, "What are we doing wrong?"

"Perhaps we need to find out what *Ginny* wants to do with her life," he replied.

"But what kind of life can she possibly have if she doesn't learn how to meet people and make better use of her abilities?"

Her husband wisely answered, "Perhaps she has some qualities and abilities that we're not aware of."

Together they decided they would show

more interest in Ginny's biology studies. They would also plan weekend outings for the family where they could get better acquainted with one another as individuals.

Following this plan, every member of the family began to have more positive experiences together. Virginia and her husband learned some important things about themselves and their children. The children became better acquainted with their parents. And all of them agreed that more and better communication ought to take place among and between them.

As her parents took more interest in her and her interests, Ginny relaxed and began to lead a more balanced social life. She didn't become homecoming queen—nor did she want to—but she is planning to attend college in the fall, and she plans to participate in some extracurricular activities.

Having fun with your teenager, sharing with him the things he likes to do or does well, may be limited by your age or physical condition. However, somewhere within his scope of interests and your range of capabilities is at least one activity in which you can participate together and in which he won't feel threatened by you. You can also express interest in all of his other activities without appearing to boss or push him.

Jack Bradshaw was typical of many busy, involved parents. He learned how to relate to his son and to rebuild his relationship with him only after they had both gone through some very difficult problems.

A successful businessman and church leader, Jack was highly respected for the example he set and the counsel he freely gave others, and as a result, he was in great demand in the community, at work, and at church. He was a very busy man—but he found little time for his family.

Jimmy, Jack's thirteen-year-old son, was the terror of the eighth grade and his Scout troop. For nearly two years, bad-conduct reports on Jimmy came to the Bradshaw home. Conferences with teachers, counselors, and other youth leaders offered no useful insights to his parents. One youth adviser did advise Jack to spend more time, in a one-on-one relationship, with his son. Jack rejected that advice. "I spend enough time with him," he claimed. "We have a good talk together every Sunday evening. I don't have time for any more than that."

One day, after Jimmy had once again disrupted a Scout activity, his concerned Scoutmaster took him aside and talked with him. He asked Jimmy about his Sunday-evening talks with his father, and the boy said, "Oh, he tells me what he'll do if I don't shape up, but he never does what he says he'll do. I don't think he really cares that much *what* I do."

The Scoutmaster decided to share with the Bradshaws some of the things he learned in his talk with Jimmy, hoping that he wouldn't at the same time jeopardize his own relationship with him. The Bradshaws, who trusted the leader and his judgment, counseled together for a long time after their meeting with him. They decided to accept his recommendation that Jack forget about threats and his son's misconduct for a time and spend more time with the boy in activities of Jimmy's choice.

Over the following weeks and months, Jack Bradshaw learned to say no to outsiders who wanted to infringe on his time. He found time to take Jimmy to football games and on fishing trips, and they even took boxing lessons together. Jack also found time for long conversations with his son—but Jimmy's problems were discussed only if he himself brought them up. As they developed mutual respect and trust, each learned a great deal about the other. The son came to know and understand his father better, and Jack learned things about Jimmy he'd never known before.

Without actually being dealt with directly, Jimmy's misconduct at school and at church rapidly decreased and then ceased. Jack wrote to the Scoutmaster who had taken such an interest in his son and expressed his gratitude that he now had a more loving, trusting relationship with Jimmy. He indicated that Jimmy had at first found it difficult to believe that Jack's interest in his activities was genuine—Jack had waited almost too long. But as a result of this experience, he was now determined to start having fun with his younger sons immediately.

Somewhere in the generation gap or in the establishment of authority in the parent-child relationship, many families lose touch with one another and start to go their separate ways. Sometimes parents forget what it was like to be a teenager—and sometimes teenagers don't realize that their parents *were* once teenagers. It's important for a teenager to see in each of his parents other facets of their personalities than those most visible as parent-authority figures. He needs to see them as teenagers who went through many of the same experiences he is now having, as persons who have matured and grown up.

Involve yourself in the interests of your teen-ager—whether it's sports, books, collecting things, raising animals, or any other kind of activity. Look for ways to share with him naturally, without forcing on him yourself and your ways of doing things. Learn what "turns him on"—and then enjoy your times together.

4

Communicating with Them

Many things of value in the world come about because someone sells something to someone else, be it an idea or a product. And the primary way to sell anything is through effective communication.

To make good things happen in your relationship with your teenager, you need to learn how to sell both yourself and your values and ideas to him. One excellent way to do this, as attested to by many parents, is through a regular personal, private interview (PPI)—a face-to-face, one-on-one conversation in a comfortable place where no one else can hear or disturb you.

Discipline sessions and one-way conversations do not qualify as PPIs. For example, Jack Bradshaw's original idea of a one-on-one session mentioned earlier was merely a discipline session—and a poor one at that. The conversations he and his son Jimmy later had during their fun times together would more appropriately be called PPIs.

Introducing the idea of a regular PPI might be done more or less directly, depending upon the relationship you already have with your teenager. If the situation is somewhat tenuous and a degree of trust has not already been established, use some caution. Be as casual as possible, and look for opportunities to be alone with him in normal surroundings and circumstances. This might be done during times when you're working together, when you're involved in a family project, or when you both find yourselves alone together in the house. If this doesn't happen naturally, look for ways to make it happen.

Once you're alone together, ask him questions that show a nonjudgmental interest in some facet of or activity in his life, or share with him some of your activities and interests. Take the time to learn about and prove your interest in the problem-free areas of his life before you help him open up on those areas that are troubling him. If you show genuine interest and affection and continue to seek opportunities to be alone with him (even doing so by appointment, if necessary), he'll eventually begin to let down his guard. Then, without any great fanfare or formal announcement, you can move into a regular (preferably weekly) personal, private interview.

Jane, who is now approaching marriage and the prospect of a family of her own, recalls the interviews she had with her father in her teenage years. "One of the things I remember most when Dad started having regular interviews was that he would try different techniques in talking with me. One technique was to repeat whatever I said, but in a different way, and then just listen to my responses. This indicated to me that he understood what I was saying and that he was willing to listen. At the same time, he was teaching me good communication skills. That same technique is important to me now as I work with younger girls in a youth program.

"When I was growing up," Jane continued,

"my parents thought I was very withdrawn and shy. Actually, I spent a lot of time thinking. If something was on my mind, I needed to think it through first before I could discuss it. Sometimes after thinking something through, I'd solve my own problem. Then I had no need to discuss it with others. Through our one-on-one discussions, my father discovered this. He was sensitive to my need to have time to think, and he was always ready to listen when I wanted to talk."

Your initial personal, private interview with your teenager may seem awkward, as may also the second and the third. But if you persist, you will eventually be able to convince him that you really do care, that you really do want to listen to him and understand him. Learn to negotiate those things that are negotiable—and to hang tough where it matters. As you improve your communication with him, you'll discover strengths and personality traits that you probably haven't seen before. You'll also probably find out that he really cares about you and what you think, and that he'll come to appreciate your wisdom and experience.

The PPI should not be reserved for problem children or only to solve behavior difficulties. Every parent and teenager can benefit from regular one-on-one sessions, even those who already seem to have a good relationship. This is what Bill Jones discovered.

Bill and his four sons enjoyed playing basketball together. In fact, they were so good that they challenged and beat every other team in town except the high school varsity team. Bill took the boys fishing, went with them to sports activities, took an interest in their schooling, attended PTA meetings, and supported them in concerts and plays in which they participated.

Money was not a problem in the Jones family, and Bill was able to fulfill the needs and wants of his sons. Always receptive to any idea that would help strengthen his family, he decided to try holding personal interviews with the boys after hearing about PPIs in a talk at church. The result was an even better relationship with each of them. Only after he began holding individual interviews did he realize that in all the time he'd spent with them, virtually none of it had been on a one-on-one basis.

If a PPI is to be successful, you need to be able to keep your teenager's confidences and to handle admissions of guilt with compassion and fairness and without anger or retribution. As he begins to

have more positive feelings about confiding in you
and exposing some of the more private areas of
his life, he might test you to see how you will react
to his small indiscretions. If you respond too
judgmentally, too negatively, or with threats of
violence or severe punishment, you will lose
ground that will be difficult or impossible to re-
cover.

Two methods of dealing with that first "testing" have proven successful for many parents:

1. Simply echo or paraphrase his statement.
For example, you might repeat, in a nonjudgmental or nonquestioning way, "You tried a bottle of
beer last week, and you're not sure if you even like
it." Don't ask it as a question; just paraphrase with
a declining inflection on the last word. Then be
quiet and let him continue. He may ask for advice;
but if he doesn't, try method number two.

2. Ask him what he thinks would be a good
solution to the problem. Discussing and agreeing
on solutions may be the only way to eventually
reach the point where you can give advice or demand compliance without rebellion.

As you deal with his faults and errors, kind-
ness is important—but so is honesty. Give him
your honest opinions, and help him find honest,
rational solutions.

The most pointless thing to do in a PPI is to simply ask a teenager how things are. The answer will probably be "fine." Ask open-ended questions, and show by your words, your inflection, and your expression that you are genuinely interested in his responses. Then listen. Try to hear the meaning behind his words.

Some teenagers are reluctant to express themselves in the presence of adults. Don't push your teenager if he doesn't talk freely at first. But watch for clues to what he is thinking as well as what he is saying. Perhaps the most important result of your first meetings together will be to reassure him that you really do care about him and are willing to give him your time, with no strings attached. One parent who was holding regular interviews with his children told me, "It doesn't make all that much difference what we talk about in the PPI, as long as it is positive rather than negative. Just showing them that I care and that I want to share my time with them does great things for their feelings of self-worth and their sense of security. And those two assurances give them calmness and self-confidence, which seems to eliminate most behavior problems."

Many teenagers feel insecure about their prospects for the future. You might lead your teen into a discussion of his hopes, dreams, and aspirations. Talk about future schooling, career opportunities, and eventual plans for marriage and family. Help him to explore new ideas and possibilities. As he shares his concerns and plans with you, listen carefully and then make notes, either mentally or in writing. Refer to your notes before future interviews to help you remember what he said and to provide openings for new ideas and concepts.

Where should the interview take place? That isn't as important as the fact that it *does* take place, as Frank Nelson discovered.

Frank, a successful salesman, spent a great deal of his time on the golf course. He enjoyed playing for relaxation as well as to meet new prospects for his business. He'd hesitate to admit it, but he also thought he needed golf to take his mind off his two sons.

Tim, Frank's eldest son, had above-average intelligence and athletic ability. Gary, two years younger than Tim, was mentally retarded. Through the years the Nelsons made genuine efforts to help Gary develop whatever potential he had, and Tim seemed to be little affected by the extra attention his brother received.

All went well until Tim reached junior high school. Then his personality began to change, almost imperceptively at first. As his friends became more aware of Gary's handicap, Tim became increasingly embarrassed, and he began to withdraw from school and church activities. By age sixteen he was overweight, lethargic, and antisocial. One day Tim's mother, in tears, told Frank, "You simply must find a way to help Tim. Everything I've tried has failed, and I don't know what to do."

Frank thought and prayed about the problem a great deal, and finally he shared it with a friend on the golf course. The friend suggested that Frank spend more time with Tim on a one-on-one basis in an activity they would both enjoy. That evening Frank offered to teach Tim to play golf, beginning the next Saturday. Thus began a process: individual attention and undivided interest for Tim; relaxing physical activity for both father and son; and light conversation as each became better acquainted with the other.

Gradually Tim became convinced that his father's interest in him was not merely superficial, and he started to confide in him and to share his innermost feelings and concerns. Frank learned of Tim's embarrassment about Gary, his shyness about girls, and his worries about his future.

Tim's problems didn't simply disappear; however, Frank found real satisfaction in discovering what was behind them and exploring ways to help Tim resolve them. As the good golfing weather disappeared in the fall, father and son continued their interviews indoors and in a more structured mode, with the enthusiastic participation and approval of both.

As you and your teenager become more relaxed in your own personal interviews, following the suggestions given in this chapter, you too should find exciting new dimensions in your own lives.

5

Helping
Them
Set
Goals

A person who sets out to go nowhere usually gets there. It's important that teenagers have goals in life. Your teenager may or may not have consciously said to himself, "That is what I want to do," or "This is what I want to be," or "These are the standards of conduct that I shall expect of myself." If he hasn't yet set such goals for himself, your interest and guidance can help him to do so. If he has set goals, your interest and concern can help him reach them.

Sometimes goals are important to young people only because they seem to be important to their parents. Most parents hope their children will turn out to be better persons than they themselves are. But parents need to be careful to help their children set their own goals, rather than simply giving them the parents' goals.

Before you can have a positive influence on the standards and goals of your teenager, you need to review your own standards and goals. What do you expect of yourself and of those with whom you associate? How well have you met your own expectations with respect to your work or interests in life? What are you doing toward achieving your goals?

If you expect your teenager to set higher goals than your own, you may have to either change your life to meet the standards you expect of him or frankly admit that you are unwilling or unable to change and that you hope he will exceed your standards. Be honest with yourself, and face the fact that the second option puts you on very shaky ground in dealing with him.

The example you set in your own life is probably the most potent teaching element to which your teenager is exposed. If "the twig is bent," it is more forcefully bent by example than by precept. Review the manner in which your life proceeds from day to day and consider such things as your language, both at home and away from home; your manner of dress; the way in which you deal with family members as well as business acquaintances and personal friends; your personal habits; your moral standards; and your integrity. Decide whether or not your standards in each area are conducive to helping your teenager set high ones for himself. Children are rarely deceived: they usually see us as we really are, not as we might wish to be seen.

When you can see yourself as you really are and have made such improvements in yourself as you are able to make, then you are ready to proceed to help your teenager set his goals. Make good use of your own strengths in influencing him positively, and be prepared to make adjustments when he sets goals and standards in areas where you are weak.

Your family and its traditions, beliefs, and practices can be a tremendous asset as you help him set his goals and standards. This applies to your immediate family, particularly if there are other children, as well as to the extended family group composed of grandparents, aunts, uncles, and cousins. The family is, after all, the basic unit of society. So much that is good is perpetuated through the family. The hopes and expectations of other family members can be extremely influential as a teenager tries to decide what to expect of himself.

While family influences and pressures may be applied positively, don't let them become obstacles. Don't hold up the standards and accomplishments of other family members as threats to your teenager, or allow them to provide negative comparisons that might erode his self-image.

In your personal interviews, try to determine how he feels about the family and its individual members—whether or not he respects their accomplishments and standards, and whether or not he cares what they think about him and what he does. If you ask him directly, he may not initially provide honest answers to these questions or reveal how important these things are to him. But if you're tactful and patient, you can lead him gently into revealing his true feelings. When you have determined the extent to which family precedents, traditions, and beliefs are important to him, you will then know how extensively you can refer to them in your personal interview discussions.

Another area in which teens need to set goals is with regard to religion and activity in church. Depending upon your teenager's personal testimony and extent of involvement, the teachings of the Church can either be a great asset or, applied too intensely or as a threat, a repellent to drive him away from you as well as the Church. It is important to help him to love God, not to fear Him. Spend more time discussing the "Thou shalts" of the gospel than the "Thou shalt nots."

If possible, become better acquainted with his church advisors and teachers and enlist them as members of your team. Don't just send your teenager to church—go with him. Discuss what happens there, and encourage him to share his feelings with you. Help him to understand that Heavenly Father loves him no less when he does wrong—that He hates the sin but loves the sinner.

Peers can have great influence on teenagers. One of the favorite arguments teens use on parents is "Everyone else does it, so why can't I?" That question is often followed by "It isn't fair." In your personal, private interviews, it's important to establish two precepts:

1. "Everybody does it" cuts no ice in your family.

2. No one ever said that life would be fair.

Establish as gently as possible the idea that others' standards are not necessarily those of your family.

Making judgments about a teenager's friends is loaded with potential problems. Although it is a parent's responsibility to make those judgments, the manner in which you reveal them is critical. If you reject his friends, in a sense you reject him also—at least he will feel that you do. If you demand that he disassociate himself from a particular friend or group of friends, you may only succeed in alienating him, and he may, in turn, intensify his friendships out of defiance.

George Pierce was faced with such a situation when his seventeen-year-old son, Bill, took up with a new friend, Brad, and began using language that was unacceptable in the Pierce household. Without thinking carefully through the problem, George simply told Bill to stay away from Brad and to clean up his language.

The following Sunday morning, George asked Bill where he'd been the previous night and with whom. Bill admitted he'd been out with

Brad—and he also told George that he didn't want to have anyone else picking out his friends for him. Bill was too big for George to punish physically, so he decided to try to reason with his son through some personal, private interviews. He found it easy to reason with his son in a nonpressured situation, and their PPIs got off to a good start.

Taking a more positive approach toward Bill's new friend, George asked nonjudgmental questions, such as, "What does Brad's father do?" and "Is Brad interested in sports?" He also suggested that Bill invite Brad over for a family activity. When Brad came to the Pierce home and began interacting with members of the family, he displayed bad manners and foul language frequently enough to embarrass Bill, and the friendship cooled.

George was wise enough to avoid using any "I told you so" tactics on his son. They simply moved on to other, more positive things. And the PPIs continued as they discussed college, girls, careers, cars, and other matters on which good father-son relationships are built.

You'll be more successful in influencing your teenager to change or break off undesirable relationships if, in your PPIs, you guide him through the process of examining the character and actions of his friends and then letting him decide for himself whether they tend to draw him toward or away from his personal goals.

You may have allies at your teenager's school and in the community that you are not aware of, such as a favorite teacher. Some sleuthing may be required to find out if this is the case and who that special individual is, but it will be worth the effort. Using such people as examples or as counseling assistants, you can motivate your teenager to set high goals and standards.

If you believe the adage "As a man thinketh, so is he," try to help your teenager to believe it also and to implement it in his life. As he decides what he wants to be and how he wants to act, help him to realize that the more intensely and consistently he thinks about those goals, the more likely he is to achieve them.

6

Disciplining
Them

The very word *discipline* has a rather harsh
connotation, with overtones of physical punishment. Perhaps a better title for this chapter would
be "Teaching Self-discipline."

Since young children are not initially capable
of self-discipline, parents need to begin teaching
them early with firm but carefully and lovingly applied disciplinary measures. Then they can move
gradually through a process of relaxing their discipline and teaching the children to discipline
themselves.

Many parents begin applying discipline with one of two strikes against them: they either use the methods their own parents used with them or, because they resented their own parents' methods, they do exactly the opposite. Going to either extreme can be harmful.

Among those who are charged with responsibility for disciplining—parents, school officials, law enforcement officers, military personnel, and so forth—those who are most successful are those whose methods are based upon concern for individuals rather than upon selfish motives. They do not pattern their discipline after examples they have seen, but simply concern themselves with the ultimate best interests of the individual.

Discipline, if properly administered, is a form of love. If you love your teenager or want to love him, discipline is necessary. Possibly the greatest harm done to children is to allow them to grow up without discipline.

Discipline plays an important part in the development of a child's emotional security. Without it, he may become unstable in his thoughts and actions, lacking the self-esteem so necessary to give balance to his life. Everyone needs to know the boundaries beyond which he cannot go without serious consequences, and discipline helps to establish those boundaries. If your teenager doesn't know where his boundaries are, he'll keep testing and looking for them until he finds them. And if you, his parent, don't establish them, the law will—usually with traumatic results.

Just as the walls of your home represent security and protection from the weather and other kinds of invasion from the outside world, so also do the protective walls of discipline represent security and protection to a teenager. To be happy and comfortable within himself, he needs some boundaries, and he ought to share in establishing them.

Some parents, with the best of intentions, make rules that are either unreasonable or unenforceable, or both. Others establish no rules at all. The best procedure is for you both to establish together the rules and regulations that will govern his activities. If he has a voice in establishing them, he'll be more inclined to respect them than to fight them. And he may even set up tougher standards than you will.

Once the boundaries or rules governing personal appearance and conduct are established, be sure that they are not stretched or ignored. If there are two parents in your home, set and enforce the rules together, and be sure your discipline is consistent.

Boundaries generally need to be set in the following areas: personal grooming and dress, manners and conduct at home and away from home, scholastics, dating, movies and other entertainment, curfew, driving, and athletics.

As you set rules and enforce them, consider these five guidelines:

1. Make no rules that are unenforceable.

2. Once a rule is made, be sure it is enforced.

3. Never discipline in anger.

4. After you have disciplined your teenager, show him great love and affection afterward. This will enhance, not lessen, the effectiveness of the discipline.

5. Be sure you understand the difference between discipline and abuse, both mental and physical. Discipline is an extension of love and concern and should never be administered abusively.

Discipline may take any of several forms, including simple parental disapproval, withholding of privileges, additional chores beyond those normally expected of the teenager, and grounding.

If your teenager has a clear understanding of

the limits and expectations as well as the consequences for exceeding the limits or failing to meet the expectations, your responsibility to discipline will be easier. The results will be even better if you and he agree in advance, through a personal interview, on the limits, expectations, and consequences.

Many teenager-parent relationships live or perish on the length of a boy's hair or a girl's skirt, or on growing a beard or using makeup. Differences between parents' and teenagers' expectations can become serious points of contention. They may result in hostility and resentment, and little learning or positive change can take place thereafter.

Such matters may be resolved through the PPI. If rational discussion takes place before rules are set and enforced, the chances are greater that they'll be observed.

On some matters, it's possible to bend a bit. After all, modes of grooming and dress come and go, with little foundation in reason. Cleanliness and neatness are important; styles and fads are not. Discuss these matters together, negotiating negotiables and "hanging tough" when it really matters.

If your teenager breaks house rules (those little day-to-day discipline problems that seem to
annoy parents, such as curfew, mealtimes, and
cleaning up his room), the answer is the same:
conduct a PPI. Angry words and shouting never
acomplish the long-range objective, though they
might halt the immediate offense.

How should you handle defiance? What
should you do if your teenager absolutely refuses
to obey or rebuffs your attempts to counsel with
him? Defiance usually has its genesis either in guilt
or in one or more previous child-parent conflicts.
The teenager may be showing resentment for
your previous judgments against him, or he may
be protecting himself against having to reveal
some mistake he has made. If you meet defiance
with anger, physical force, or threats, you might
never find out what is behind the defiance. You
may succeed in overpowering or intimidating
him, but you won't solve the basic problem, and
defiance will occur again when he feels he has the
power to back it up.

Power, rather than love, often becomes the
central theme in parent-child relationships. When
that happens (the familiar term is "power strug-
gle"), regardless of who wins any particular battle,
ultimately no one wins.

Once you've established a pattern of negotiating disciplinary matters, you'll find that reasonable solutions to most problems can be reached. For example, the age at which he is allowed to date and rules he should observe in dating can be established after you have agreed on some basic principles and groundrules.

School and scholastic expectations, driving, rules for watching TV, guidelines for selecting movies to see—all of these matters differ from family to family. Each one can be resolved in a personal interview, if the discussion is based on love and concern for the long-range well-being of the teenager.

If you love him, you will discipline him. But be consistent, firm, and fair. And always let your love for him be the basis of all discipline.

7

Trusting Them

Trust is an important element in the relationship between parent and teenager. However, if absolutes are applied in defining *trust* or in the expectations parents have for their teenagers, disappointment and disillusionment often enter in. All of us—parents as well as teens—are human and, therefore, make mistakes. We all fail at times to reach our usual standard of performance, as this dialogue shows:

Son: What's the matter, Dad—don't you trust me?

Dad: Sure, son—I trust you to be human, young, and not yet perfect. Therefore, you'll make mistakes.

Your relationship with your teenager should not stand or fall on a single failure of either of you to meet the usual level of performance. If you can establish in a private interview with him that you both make mistakes but that you'll both do your best to be consistently faithful to established expectations, your relationship should weather most of the storms that will come.

Trust between parents and teenagers needs to be built and strengthened over a period of time and on the basis of each being consistently trustworthy.

Your teenager, for example, should be able to trust you to keep confident any private matters he reveals to you. By the same token, you should trust him to carry out any commitments that he makes with you. In either case, that trust should continue until good cause is shown why it should not continue.

If suspicions develop that trust is being violated, the suspected violator should be given opportunity to explain his actions before final conclusions are drawn and others are involved.

Sometimes just one slip can undo a lifetime of trust. That's what happened to Miriam Johnson and her thirteen-year-old daughter, Bonnie. The Johnsons live in a small town where everyone seems to know everything about everyone else. Bonnie and her mother were very good friends, and they always felt free to talk to each other and to share confidences.

Miriam's friend Carol also had a thirteen-year-old daughter, Francine. Carol admired Miriam and enjoyed hearing her tell about her special relationship with Bonnie. She tried to emulate Miriam, since she didn't feel as comfortable in her own relationship with Francine.

Miriam hadn't anticipated the need for confidentiality in her talks with Bonnie when boys became the number one interest in Bonnie's life. One day in the hallway at school, Francine, in a mocking tone, said to Bonnie, "I hear you've got a crush on Todd Andrews."

"Who told you that?" Bonnie demanded. It was not difficult for her to trace the route of the information from Francine through Carol and back to her mother, Miriam.

Miriam Johnson learned a painful lesson from that experience. An apology, many months of rebuilding, and many more personal talks were required before Bonnie's trust in her mother was restored.

Confidences shared in private should be kept sacred if open communication between you and your teenager is to continue. Learn to trust him—and respect his right to complete trust in you in turn.

8

Encouraging Their Independence

One of the paradoxes of raising teenagers is illustrated by the comment, "He says he's in love and wants to get married and be a father, but he hasn't learned yet to pick up his dirty socks."

Every teenager needs to learn to make his own decisions—when to go to bed, when to get up, when to go on dates, when to come home from dates, whether or not to go on an overnight trip out of town, when to take the car, what kind of movies to watch, whether or not to grow a beard, whether to study or go out for pizza. Decisions that his parents have made for him in the past, he now needs and wants to make for himself. That desire is not intrinsically bad. As a matter of fact, it's good. Timing is the key.

Everyone has to learn eventually to make his own decisions, and it helps if parents think back to their own experiences. One father who now has four children remembers how, when he was about ten, he used to enjoy playing with other neighborhood children in the evening. "At about nine o'clock," he recalls, "several of us had to go home. A few remained, bragging that they could stay out as late as they wished. I was envious, thinking of the good times they'd still be having while I was lying in bed.

"As the years went by, I noticed differences between those who had had to leave early and those who stayed late. The children who stayed late were allowed by their parents to make many decisions about their conduct and activities much earlier than we were. But I see now, in retrospect, that they were often the ones who had discipline and personality problems as teenagers and young adults. As a rule, we who were given decision-making privileges more gradually had a relatively trouble-free childhood and adolescence and have become well-adjusted adults."

In order to mature properly and to ultimately become responsible adults, every teenager must learn to make decisions. His parents' responsibility is to see that he makes decisions that challenge him, promote the desired growth in his character, and reassure him that he is becoming the master of his fate, the captain of his soul. At the same time, they must ensure that he doesn't become overwhelmed by decisions he is not prepared to handle. Failure in decision making can be traumatic, just as success can be stimulating.

As you turn decision-making power over to your teenager, it's wise to start cautiously. Some matters, though they may seem important to him, are not of great consequence in the long run, such as dress and hair style and some household rules. You might make him *responsible* for those decisions rather than simply giving him total control without accountability. One parent explained, "I trust my kids, but I check on them. That way I can continue to trust them. How can I know when it's time to give them larger decisions to make if I don't know how they're handling the smaller ones?"

Teenagers need to understand that they can earn more decision-making power if they are rational and consistent in the decisions they have been entrusted to make. Discuss with your teenager decisions he has made, and continue to give him enough decisions to keep him interested and challenged but not overwhelmed.

John Franklin, a teacher, had reasonable success in rearing his own four teenagers as well as in teaching others. He once asked a group of teenagers two questions: "How many of you feel you are allowed to make enough of your own decisions?" and "How many of you feel you don't make enough of your own decisions?" He was surprised—and pleased—to learn that most of the teenagers were satisfied with their decision-making privileges. He noted, however, that some did not respond at all until he asked, "How many of you get to make too many decisions?" A few raised their hands.

John wondered how parents would respond to the question, "Does your teenager have too little, enough, or too much freedom in decision making?" He surmised that half the parents' answers would match the answers of their children. He also believed that when the parents' answers did *not* match their children's answers, those parents probably did not have regular, one-on-one communication with their teenagers.

Remember that one day you'll send your child off into the world, where he'll have to make virtually all of his own decisions. Perhaps he won't still be a teenager, but he'll probably still be somewhat unsure of himself. He'll handle that challenge better if you have led him carefully down the decision-making road to the point where he has been making most of his own decisions before the day when he moves out of your home.

As you help him develop his decision-making abilities, let him know often that you love him and have confidence in him. If you repeat these assurances on that special day when he moves out on his own, you'll strengthen immeasurably his ability to establish with confidence his independence as an adult.

9

Helping
Them
Overcome
Evil

Tobacco, liquor, drugs, and premarital sex. If these four temptations were magically removed from existence, many parents would feel that they could take extended vacations from parenting. In terms of the traumas created in the lives of teenagers and their parents, these four evils should logically be handled in many volumes, not just a short chapter in a small book.

I've chosen, however, to write briefly about them for a reason that may appear very simplistic, but that is, I believe, nevertheless true. That reason is: *Problems among teenagers with tobacco, liquor, drugs, and premarital sex are not causes—they are effects.* That is, they are symptoms or external manifestations of defects in parental teaching, in the teenager's self-image, or in the parent-child relationship, or a combination of these elements.

In order to give helpful advice, I am assuming that the standard that parents wish to establish with their teenagers is one that precludes involvement with those evils. If that standard has been taught before a child reaches his teens and he then violates it, the root of the violation may be:

1. The temptation is stronger than the teachings and example given in the home.

2. The teenager's self-image is weaker than the pressure applied by peers.

3. The teenager resents his parents and is rebelling in order to repay them for wrongs he feels they have done him.

When asked about his ability to deal with the temptations of the world, a young adult said emphatically, "I love my parents very much. Nothing could hurt me more than to disappoint them. This has kept me from experimenting with drugs, liquor, and premarital sex. Whenever I've been tempted, I've thought about my parents."

If high standards concerning these things have not been fostered and taught in your home, and if your teenager has not picked up such standards somewhere else, your work is cut out for you. Communication needs to be established between you. However, you should also be aware that your chances of achieving complete success are not good.

Let's look at the three root causes mentioned earlier and see how they might be handled.

1. *The temptation is stronger than the teachings and example given in the home.*

If, despite your teaching, your teenager has succumbed to evil temptations, you must show him unconditional love. Assure him through hugs, kisses, and words that you love him even though you abhor his sin. He needs to know how important he is to you and how much you want him to have the very best things in life.

Communication is the major key to helping him avoid or overcome temptation. Try to increase the frequency of your private talks with him. Lead him into sharing his thoughts and feelings by making nonthreatening statements, such as, "You seem to enjoy drinking with your friends." Then let him talk. Listen closely for clues to what he is really saying. Only then will you discover ways to help him counter the strong forces that are working against your teachings. When he begins to reveal his true inner feelings and motivations, you can use your own natural wisdom and insight as a parent to counsel him.

2. *The teenager's self-image is weaker than the pressure applied by peers.*

Some teenagers become involved with tobacco, liquor, drugs, or premarital sex for no other reason than to achieve parity with their peers. Perhaps your teenager feels inferior in some way to persons his own age whom he admires or with whom he would like to associate. If they are involved in activities that are contrary to the standards established in your home, he may feel that he has to become involved in order to gain their acceptance. That kind of peer pressure is one of the most difficult problems to handle. At times, the need for acceptance by peers can be stronger than any other influence in his life.

The best solution would be to help raise him above the need for approval of his peers, to help him build his self-image so that his strength comes from within himself rather than from acceptance by others.

Begin by analyzing his character, personality,

and special abilities. Everyone has some quality, ability, or potential that deserves praise or can be built up so that it does. The object is to find that special quality and then talk with him about it, encourage him in it, and help him build it up. You may then go from one characteristic or ability to another, reinforcing each one, until he sees himself as being very special, as a child of God who has great abilities and potential.

You probably won't see a real change in his self-image in a short time, but be patient. It can be done. As his parent, you can probably help him best because you know him best. But don't overlook opportunities to involve others—friends, teachers, advisers, and associates. Enlist their aid in helping him build and strengthen his self-esteem. Encourage him to associate with peers who will influence well and will strengthen him. Your chances of success will multiply with each new direction from which positive appraisals and encouragement come to him.

3. *The teenager resents his parents and is rebelling in order to repay them for wrongs he feels they have done him.*

If your teenager's involvement with harmful substances or premarital sex is rooted in a display of open rebellion, it might well be time for self-analysis—for *you*. Have you caused his resentment through your methods of discipline? Have you been too authoritarian or inconsistent? Have you been hypocritical, expecting more of him than of yourself? Have you treated him in some way worse than you've treated another member of the family?

You have taken a good first step when you have analyzed the situation and identified your own shortcomings or failings in your relationship with him. If your behavior needs correcting, start now to work on it.

As with other problems in rearing teenagers, communication is vital if you are to achieve success. And as with the other problems discussed in this book, a personal, private interview is a good place to start. As you work to reestablish open communication with your teenager, admit your own mistakes. Give him the opportunity to forgive you. Have him help you set some short-term goals for yourself based upon mutually set standards. If you are sincere in your efforts to change yourself, you may soon see him starting to change himself and his own attitudes.

To illustrate some of these principles, let's look at the experience of Pete Williams.

Pete had been raised on a cattle ranch, where he and his four brothers helped their father on the range. Their mother died shortly after Pete was born, and their father applied discipline to his sons in the only way he knew—a sharp word followed by a cuff about the ears if that didn't work.

Pete and his wife had a sixteen-year-old son, Larry, and two younger daughters. Pete left the training of the girls to his wife and handled Larry in much the same way as his own father had handled him. Two things were different, however: Pete and his family didn't live on a ranch, and Larry was not a cowboy, but an outstanding athlete on a high school wrestling team.

During Larry's junior year in high school, as his athletic prowess improved, he began to adopt some of the habits of other athletes at school—swearing, talking crudely about girls, and using liquor and tobacco. One of Pete's friends owned a grocery store, and from him Pete learned that an adult had purchased a case of beer for Larry and his friends. He also learned that the youths used very offensive language whenever they came into the store.

That night Pete went to Larry's room and confronted him with the grocer's report. Larry said little and denied none of the accusations. Pete angrily demanded, "It had better never happen again!"

"What will you do about it if it does?" Larry retorted.

Pete cuffed him sharply on the side of his head and shouted, "This—and a lot more!"

Larry took a step backward, stood at his full height—two inches taller than his father—and said menacingly, "If you ever do that again, I'll hit back."

As father and son glared at each other, Pete suddenly realized that he was no longer able to physically control his son. He muttered, "We'll see," and left the room.

For several days Pete couldn't make any sense out of the frustration, anger, and parental concern he felt. Finally he overcame his pride and confided in his wife. "Maybe you're more concerned about your image as a good, strict parent than you are about finding the solution to Larry's problem," she responded. Together they discussed how Pete might reopen the door to communication with his son. They decided that some one-on-one conversation was needed—with Larry allowed to do at least half of the talking.

Pete's first private interview with Larry wasn't

a success, because Larry expected a lecture, while Pete expected Larry to open up to him. Neither, of course, happened. Pete did manage, however, to apologize to Larry, saying, "I guess I'm still treating you like a little kid, and you're not a little kid anymore." They agreed to start over again in a few days.

At the second interview session, Pete guided the conversation through wrestling, school courses, college plans, girls, friends, peer pressure, and other concerns Larry might have.

Over the next year they continued their discussions. Few changes took place in Larry's attitudes and actions during that year, and at times Pete found it necessary to apply such measures as curtailing Larry's use of the family car and giving him extra chores around the house. These disciplinary actions were always discussed in the private interview sessions, and Larry agreed to them without strong resentment. Sometimes he even remarked, "I deserved that."

Gradually the father and son became friends, and their discussions began to turn in the direction of what Larry wanted to be and to do rather than what Pete expected of him. And gradually Larry began to control his language as well as his use of alcohol and tobacco when he found that they didn't fit the goals he had set for himself.

Teenagers' use of tobacco, liquor, drugs, and other harmful substances, and their indulgence in premarital sex, all present enormous concern and challenges to parents, to schools, to churches, and to law enforcement agencies. Information and counseling relative to the harmful effects of these substances and practices are readily available, and these are somewhat helpful. But they treat the symptoms rather than the causes. The real problems will disappear, I believe, only when the causes are treated through more effective communication between parents and their children.

10

Building
Their
Self-Image

For many people, life is an unending search. Currently popular are phrases about "finding myself," "getting my head on straight," "seeking my true identity," "learning to be my own person." Some use such expressions to rationalize desertion of their families or abandonment of other responsibilities. Others may not go to such drastic extremes, but nevertheless fail to achieve their expectations and potential. Often the cause is poor self-image.

Parents have a great influence—perhaps the greatest influence—on the development of the self-image of children. They can help their children build a strong and healthy self-image— but they may also cause that self-image to be damaged or destroyed.

To help build a strong self-image in your child, you won't accomplish much by using a "play-it-by-ear and hope-for-the-best" approach. A contractor who hopes to build a strong building, an attorney who hopes to build a strong case, an administrator who hopes to build a strong organization—each must follow a plan. And so must a parent who wants to help build and strengthen his child's self-image.

Elizabeth, a happy, well-adjusted young adult, remembers how her parents helped her. "Dad and Mom concentrated on positive things," she recalls. "Dad was a counselor, and he'd come to me for help with a lesson he was preparing or a special message for the children of a family he was counseling. He'd tell me I had a talent for working with children and for thinking of clever ideas to hold their attention.

"Mom was active in a woman's organization, and she'd ask me for help in arranging flowers or preparing relish trays for her seminars. She'd always praise me for the little things I did. My parents' praise and confidence in me really influenced the development of my self-image."

An important step in planning how to help your teenager build his self-image is to examine your relationship with him. For example, does he love and respect you? If so, your approval or disapproval of him and his actions can dramatically influence the development of his feelings toward himself. That doesn't mean that you must approve of everything he does. It simply means that you must be cautious in expressing approval or disapproval, realizing the impact it could have on him.

Too much approval might cause him to be over-confident. Too little approval or too much disapproval might cause him to lose confidence in himself and to seek companions whose standards and behavior are not as high as those of his family. If he can't find sufficient status in his relationship with you, he will seek it from others, and he may resort to unacceptable behavior in order to get it. This is frequently the point at which teenagers start experimenting with alcohol, tobacco, drugs, and premarital sex.

If that happens with your teenager, re-member that the problem is not with the evils themselves. The problem is probably in his re-lationship with you or in his self-image—or both. And the solution to the problem lies in reestablish-ing communication between you in a positive, nonjudgmental way.

As you seek to help your teenager through this difficult period, temper your approval on oc-casion with reminders that he is less than perfect and will, therefore, make mistakes. Then temper your disapproval with reminders that you truly love him, that your love is unconditional, and that he does have admirable qualities.

Since developing a healthy self-image in your teenager is more likely to happen by plan than by accident, determine some of the concepts you want to help instill in him. For example, you may wish to help him recognize that

1. He is lovable and he is loved.

2. He is an intelligent being, capable of ra-tional thinking, and can therefore make sensible decisions.

3. He is physically acceptable to others, re-gardless of any physical handicap he may have.

4. He has both strengths and weaknesses,

and he can develop his strengths and learn to minimize or overcome his weaknesses.

5. He is a child of God, a person of real worth and value.

As you endeavor to plant those concepts in his mind, talk with him and treat him in such a way as to assure him they are true. Try to make each experience of his life a reinforcement of one or more of those concepts, and use your one-on-one private-interview time with him to build on them.

As you think of your teenager, so is he likely to think of himself. And as he thinks of himself, so is he likely to become!